Our Holidays

Celebrate
Christmas

Elizabeth Lawrence

Cavendish
Square

New York

Published in 2016 by Cavendish Square Publishing, LLC
243 5th Avenue, Suite 136, New York, NY 10016

First Edition

Website: cavendishsq.com

This publication represents the opinions and views of the author based on his or her personal experience, knowledge, and research. The information in this book serves as a general guide only. The author and publisher have used their best efforts in preparing this book and disclaim liability rising directly or indirectly from the use and application of this book.

CPSIA Compliance Information: Batch #WS15CSQ

All websites were available and accurate when this book was sent to press.

Library of Congress Cataloging-in-Publication Data

Lawrence, Elizabeth.
Celebrate Christmas / by Elizabeth Lawrence.
p. cm. — (Our holidays)
Includes index.
ISBN 978-1-50260-407-1 (hardcover)
ISBN 978-1-50260-406-4 (paperback)
πISBN 978-1-50260-408-8 (e-book)
1. Christmas — Juvenile literature. I. Lawrence, Elizabeth, 1988-. II. Title.
GT4985.5 L366 2016
394.2663—d23

Editorial Director: David McNamara
Editor: Kristen Susienka
Copy Editor: Cynthia Roby
Art Director: Jeffrey Talbot
Designer: Joseph Macri
Senior Production Manager: Jennifer Ryder-Talbot
Production Editor: Renni Johnson

Printed in the United States of America

Contents

Today is Christmas.

Christmas is on December 25.

4

DECEMBER

Sunday	Monday	Tuesday	Wednesday	Thursday	Friday	Saturday
1	2	3	4	5	6	7
8	9	10	11	12	13	14
15	16	17	18	19	20	21
22	23	24	25	26	27	28
29	30	31				

Many people **celebrate** Christmas to remember when Jesus was born.

7

Christmas is a time for being with family and friends.

We make cookies.

There are many **traditions** at Christmas.

One tradition is to **decorate** a Christmas tree.

11

Another tradition is that **Santa Claus** brings presents on Christmas.

13

We leave Santa Claus cookies and milk.

14

15

On Christmas, families give presents to each other, too.

We also sing Christmas carols together.

Christmas is a special holiday.

Merry Christmas!

New Words

celebrate (SELL-uh-brate) To observe an event in some special way.

decorate (DEK-or-ate) To make an object look nice by painting, drawing, or putting other objects, such as ribbons or glitter, on it.

Santa Claus (SAN-tuh KLAWZ) A man with a bushy white beard who dresses in red during Christmas. He brings presents.

traditions (tra-DIH-shunz) Events you do every year during holidays, such as baking cookies or singing Christmas carols.

22

Index

About the Author

Elizabeth Lawrence lives in Albany, New York. She likes to write books, celebrate holidays with family and friends, and cook.

About BOOKWORMS

Bookworms help independent readers gain reading confidence through high-frequency words, simple sentences, and strong picture/text support. Each book explores a concept that helps children relate what they read to the world in which they live.